D0887899

And God Said:
Let there be Evolution!

Karen —

thanks so much
for coming out!

Steve H

Other Books by Steve Henn

Unacknowledged Legislations, NYQ Books, 2010

And God Said:
Let there be Evolution!

Steve Henn

The New York Quarterly Foundation, Inc.
New York, New York

NYQ Books™ is an imprint of The New York Quarterly Foundation, Inc.

The New York Quarterly Foundation, Inc.
P. O. Box 2015
Old Chelsea Station
New York, NY 10113

www.nyqbooks.org

Copyright © 2012 by Steve Henn

All rights reserved. No part of this book may be used or reproduced in any manner whatsoever without written permission of the author except in the case of brief quotations embodied in critical articles and reviews. This book is a work of fiction.

First Edition

Set in New Baskerville

Layout and Design by Raymond P. Hammond
Cover Illustration by Pete Tuura

Library of Congress Control Number: 2012941098

ISBN: 978-1-935520-62-7

And God Said:
Let there be Evolution!

Acknowledgments

Some of these poems previously appeared in the chapbook *Showstoppers:20 poems from the Midwest Poetry All Stars,* Superiority Complex Press, 2010.

Thanks to the editors of the following magazines and online journals where the following poems appeared:

"God's Formative Years"—*Barbaric Yawp*
"Margaret Hires a Personal Thinker"—*MFA/MFYou* (website)
"Questions from the 33rd Hearing of the Associated Writing Programs Unpoetic Activities Committee"—*Blue Collar Review*
"Pig Spill"—*Barbaric Yawp*
"Drinking Song"—*Chiron Review*
"I'm from Indiana"—*Bloomington Writer's Guild website*

and thanks to the editors of a handful of print and online journals who wouldn't touch poems about religious belief with a ten foot pole. A six foot pole? A six inch pole. Maybe with a six inch pole. I'm a disturbed young man with a tan. Torturing myself. With problems so deep. And so personal. Et cetera. (Apologies to Richard Linklater.)

May God have Mercy on us all.
Like, really.
This time especially.

for Oren Wagner
the peeriest of my peers

Contents

ix

"Christianity is no different from any other cult—it isn't about faith. It's about agreement, about like-minded people sitting together in the same room at the same time believing the same thing. That unity is its appeal."

–Sarah Vowell

Do I contradict myself?
Very well then I contradict myself,
(I am large, I contain multitudes.)

—Walt Whitman

And God Said:

Let there be Evolution!
and saw that it was good. "And
may all the beasts of the land
survive through natural selection.
And may Man be given
the Divine Spark
at the appointed time."

And Science said "Rising
from the dead?
Why not?
Ever hear of String Theory?
That is some way-out shit."

And Christ came back and said
"Heaven is a parallel universe
where I've been all these years,
and Mankind is capable of destroying
or rejuvenating the Earth."

And what Marx really said was
"It's good we have religion.
It kills the pain. Like opium."

And Kurt Vonnegut Jr. noted that in a speech,
and he also said why not put
the Sermon on the Mount on the Courthouse lawn,
instead of the Ten Commandments?

And Pat Robertson didn't want to be left out
so he proclaimeth, "I know what God's thinking!"

And God said, "Pat...the hell you do."

Acrobats at the Laundromat and Incidents Less Noteworthy

Our neighbor bought a new John Deere
after pushmowing his immaculate lawn once weekly
without fail for 32 years. In celebration of
his own good taste he mowed 3 times
in the first 8 days of ownership.
I once bought a drum set which if I
were in a Shakespearean play I'd claim
to play passingly well except
after any jam session everybody didn't get married
and everybody didn't die. I had to watch
the tuning instructional video then get help
from the bass player, and a kid
I admitted this to understood immediately
why I'm an English teacher, not a rock musician.
When you've got a hobby supreme adequacy
is the only way to go otherwise somebody older
who feels washed up will tell you, "You should
do something with this!" But doing things
is always less fun than the anticipation
of doing things, so why is my neighbor
constantly scratching his mowing itch
like a compulsive masturbator?
Displacement, I bet—he's satisfying
an urge to grow pot by tending to a sparkling lawn.
That's all right. I read poetry in bars
to satisfy an urge to feel like the rock star
I'm not on the drums, and try not to think
of how rarely the experience measures up
to the anticipation.

catholic ruminations

Is Christ resurrected? That depends
on what day you ask me.
Sunday, I tend to go with the crowd.
Shout the loudest, hold a banner end
like Julia in *1984*, a safe sheep.
Mondays I can't think about it, Sunday having
exhausted me. Tuesdays I experience
a general sense of malaise, absentmindedly
taking 40 minute showers after work.
Sighing a lot and wishing for a beer.
Wednesdays I read books about crazy
physical theories like Superstring and
Gravity Doesn't Exist—on those days
why the hell not? Thursdays I'll ask
you back: what does "is" mean? Fridays
are generally for drinking or
family movie night or falling asleep
in a chair at 8:30 pm if I played ball
at 5 that morning. Saturdays I reserve
for thinking about how I'm long overdue
for confession, which I do
in my head without the aid of a priest.
It's altogether less satisfying,
like having sex with yourself, Sunday drives
by my pasture at 25 mph on a
county road 45, a small child called Faith
sticking her head out the window bellowing
"Jesus is Risen! Mooo!" as I ruminate roadside
on wild grass and the odor of global warming
coming out of my butt, the scent of it like
a last confidence well before I reach the slaughterhouse.
He may or may not be risen, but surely He died
for skipped oil changes, for savoring anger
for lobster on a Friday in Lent,
for each and every one of our godforsaken sins.

Humor Is Funny

I asked the stylist at Great Clips
if she was qualified to do the beard trim
advertised above the photo of a man
entirely too happy to be modeling for
a low end haircutting franchise
and she said "yeah" and didn't laugh and I said
"'cause I've never had it done professionally
and I have pretty high expectations"
and she said "we just go over it with the guard"
like a bored prostitute at a Vegas brothel
annoyed with a rookie John. I felt like
Mark Twain traipsing around Turkey
in search of the mythical Turkish shave
which he finally got from a muscled barber
with a Rollie Fingers moustache who scraped him raw
and stabbed him in the neck. My beard trim
was more of a metaphorical stabbing
although while cutting my hair she did nick
the back of my head and say "sorry for stabbing you
with my fingernail." She didn't do most
of the moustache so when I got home
and looked in the mirror I saw Wilford Brimley
staring back at me, then I noticed
the whole time I wore a shirt depicting
a cow telling a gallon of milk
"Milk, I am your father" to which
the milk responds "Nooooooo"
so I figured the stylist, who treated my head hair
and the accompanying person like a meter maid
sent in to write her a ticket
was one of those people who doesn't think humor is funny.

Questions for the Parishioner Who Wants Me To Join the Knights of Columbus

As in Ohio? Or the discoverer
of the already-inhabited Americas?
"Knights of Leif Ericson"—your rivals?
Or Knights of the Bering Strait Landbridge Crossers?
Be honest: are you guys one of those
dirty old mens' organizations, like the Shriners?
Who ask twentysomething lady bartenders if
they're wearing any underwear? Are you
wearing any underwear? How would you like me
to react if you say "no"? If I admit
I doubt, stand up at a club meeting,
proclaim that ticking tenets off a list
until I'm fully Orthodox is an insane,
Orwellian even, approach to religion,
would you excommunicate me
from the club? Could you, even—
from the Church? Should I fear you,
your secret handshakes, your jesusfish drawn
with sidewalk chalk on the tip of your cane,
a sign of devotion and solidarity
for co-conspirators? Have I been reading
too much Dan Brown? Hey, shouldn't child molesting
priests have their nuts cut off? What about
those get-ups you guys wear during masses
that are apparently special occasions, the plumed hats,
the sabers and faux-British dress up tops?
If I join, do I get to wear one? All the time?
Do you get to joust? If I offer up
all my valor and bravery in Wednesday night
church pick up hoops to a Fair Lady,
let's say someone in the Knights Ladies Auxiliary,
let's say your wife, in the medieval way
of chivalry and courtly love, given that it would be
platonic, idealized, nonsexual, do you think
the Bishop would have a problem with that?
Would you?

After seeing "WaRnINg: May bE dAnGERouS to KNOW mE" in individual stick-on letters in two spots on the back windows of a 1970s Chevy Suburban...in Indiana...in 2010

You mean, like, in the Biblical sense? Why not—
"My bed is a disease ridden graveyard." Isn't that more poetic?
Or Dangerous to know all about you? As in, pssst, that's
Chet, he had sex with an alpaca in 1987, but
don't tell anybody I told you, he said he'd shoot me
for it." Or is "knowing" some sort of act of
intellectual violence, like when your stepdad
or your teachers tried to Learn Ya' Good?
Do you have this message up on your profile
on Match.com, right next to a picture of your neck tattoo?
Or are you trying to ward off know-it-all evil spirits
who spend days in Purgatory humiliating the inmates
in endless games of Jeopardy? Is knowing you
more Dangerous than crossing the street blindfolded?
More Dangerous than ejaculating into a stranger?
Or vice-versa? Or is it only Dangerous in theory,
like Marxist Literary Criticism, or drinking whiskey
when you've got the beat down bottom blues?

Collect Call to the Afterworld

You have a collect call from (*me*)
in Indiana. Not Denmark, but still
like a prison. So what, you must have
neverending wildflower fields,
ambidextrous dinner tables,
VIPs on the right? Or 76 virgins
times tens of suicide bombers?
Somehow, I doubt it. Not all of it.
Not the existence of it. Just the idea
that anybody knows what the hell
they have coming. Speaking of,
do the good place and the bad place
exist side by side, like sister cities?
Or inside each other, like parallel
universes. Universi? Universum?
Who's to know what to call them,
or you. I'll go with "Olaf."
I've heard whispers of mystical battles
between angels and demons. Of a man
who animates insects from dirt.
How much of anything can we know
to be true? But you, Olaf, are the destination
of all of us, that's true. Barring divinity,
intervention by Divinity, and defibrillators,
everybody gets a one-way ticket.

I can't wait to get old

and wear cardigans every day
and not get laughed at for it, anymore
and dismount the wild horses of my annoying libido

and say whatever I want
     to the grocery store clerk
          as I buy Polident and Metamucil
     to the fuel station cashier
          as I drive the last gas-powered vehicle in America
     to the Post Office worker
          as I blame him for editors' tardy replies
     to the rookie cop one quarter my age,
          who pulls me over for doing 25 in a 70

I can't wait to get old
     and terribly nearsighted
     until all I can do is read large print books
     and demand that the tv be turned off, or
     at least up, like, 40 decibels

I can't wait to get old
     and draw my teacher's retirement pension
     and the social security benefits that will kick in
          at age 93,
               or never

I can't wait to get old
     and curse out loud whenever I want
     when my favorite prank will be wandering into
     a Walmart backaisle pretending to be confused
     shouting "Please help me! I can't
          feel my dick!"

I can't wait to get old and teach my daughters' sons
        to be sensitive poet types
            who wear funny hats
            who smoke cigarettes limpwristed
            who cry after their first kiss
            who fall in and out of love
                over and over
                    like an 8-year-old cannonballing
                    into the deep end again and again
            who mercilessly make fun of guys who
                frequent strip bars and then
                duck before they get punched

I can't wait to get old and go to strip bars
        so I can make fun of the stupidest way to spend money
            known to man
        so I can buy a 75 dollar beer at 2055 inflated prices
        and go "what the hell am I doing here anyway?"
        in garbled old man speech, which will come out
            "Whiggundissempickledammit—Huh?
                Jee-Zuzz Carimonie!"

I can't wait to get old
        so I can threaten to beat the crap out of anyone
        and nobody will hit me for it

I can't wait for titanium hips
        ivory dentures and ear hair that never stops

I can't wait to get old so I can only do things
        that I feel are worth the time (what little I have left)

I can't wait to get old because
        only then will I never again
        be afraid
            to die.

God's Formative Years

God founded mammals
so Placentas could roam the fields
lowing with pleasure, spitting up
their greasy cud. Marsupials were invented
in God's tweener years, after
a sophomoric "pocket pool" joke.
For 3 months of 15 God was so emo
he only brought forth weeping willows,
which withered pitifully in the presence
of His stepfather. A few tough, older Gods,
rough Gods, would call God Poindexter
because of his penny loafers, terrorizing Him
with feinting fists. The truth is
God was a poor, timid, bookish God—
a God without friends, a God who spoke
to girls ineffectually, who never left
the basement Friday nights. God
had no father. The Son a street stray
unceremoniously and unofficially and temporarily adopted,
fed sticks of chewing gum from the five and dime;
when He bored of the Boy He left Him
to the Romans, forsaken.

Reasons why California M.D.s have granted medical marijuana licenses

Corns, crabs, a bad back,
warts of all kinds, tendinitis of the knee, tennis elbow,
psoriasis sissy syndrome and sister love,
a bad case of existential angst,
a bad case of atheism, a bad case of jesuslove,
unexplained collect calls from the dearly departed,
undead dreadlocks, doily swirly,
mania, lack of mania, obsessive desire
for a manic state, states rights, sillynose,
acne, herpes, newsie-groupies,
unanticipated erections or the lack thereof,
off her game, too much in the zone,
DUI, DOA, DVD RSVP,
no sanctuary, no faith, no soul,
nasal drip, droopy eyelids,
douchebaggery of all varieties,
unemployed, embarrassingly endowed,
misunderstood, overqualified,
uninitiated, and in-the-know.

Political Will

As a 21st century American
expected to be indignant
about something, let me say
my Irish grandmothers never believed
in Lucky Charms, marshmallows
being an abomination
to those connoisseurs of Cream of Wheat
and Malt-O-Meal. I'm also mad
that nobody's created Indian
Trickster Crunch, because
Native Americans seem to have had
a pretty easy time of it lately,
what with the casinos
and every hillbilly from here
to Wabatucky proudly claiming "injun blood."
Our inefficient government
also angers me, run by all those
self-serving egotistical hypocrites
because that's a new development.
It's not like principled politicians died out
with Abe Lincoln I mean Thomas
Jefferson I mean Socrates.
Grrrrr, why can't people
in this town I mean this state
I mean women I mean illegals
I mean highly domesticated exotic pets
use their turn signal?
Why can't the world be
entirely the way God intended it
for me?

An Insignificant Request

Just once at a poetry reading
I'd like someone to throw their panties
at me. It wouldn't have to be a
supermodel. It could be a dude.
It could be a really old dude.
The panty-thrower would have to be of legal age
assuming 18 is legal panty-throwing age
not because I'm taking the tosser back
to my hotel room for an energetic bonk
and a whiskey-fueled smashing of furniture,
but because I am a public school teacher
and married to boot and the slightest whiff
on the wind of improper dealings with a minor
would get me fired not to mention divorced.
And that wind-whiff would smell of jasmine,
sandalwood, and bacon. You could even throw your panties
right now, if you want, or at the next reading
when we'll all pretend we've never heard this poem before
and it'll be more spontaneous and less awkward.
Already I know it's not going to happen
because nobody it happens to goes begging for it
Bret Michaels and Slash and Tommy Lee being awash
in panties at every performance and Vince Neil rumored
to hate nothing more than panties in the face
when he's shouting at the devil or otherwise vocalizing
which is a name for utterance more than speech
but not, strictly speaking, as melodic as song should be.
But please know this testimony is true
when I tell you I will utter words of thanksgiving,
words of praise, I will hold them aloft kiss them
like the Stanley Cup and exclaim throatily
with agitated joy that we are all beautiful
and nothing can stop us now if you throw your panties at me.

Sectarian Politics

"They're going to sit on that porch
in those rusty chairs all summer, watching?"
my wife says. "Judging us," I say.
"And praying for us," she hopes.
But I know people like them.
Their version of Christianity 30% prayer
65% judging and 5% miscellaneous.
Early Monday mornings counting the brown bottles
in our recycling bin. Because we are
drinking Catholic Christians and they are
Billy Sunday evangelists. Who will suggest
the right kind of Bible school for our children.
Who hear us raging at those children and cluck
knowingly of how unfull we are of God's love.
Who will warn new neighbors to hold
their belly buttons when passing our house,
as if it consists of a graveyard for souls.

After B. Hicok's "To Find the New World"

Who is this guy with the nose
and the mouth and the two eyes, eyes
that even now compare the shade of my forehead
to almonds, so predictable, these men,
would-be wooers or whatever,
almonding my skin, my eyes, almonding my secret parts,
let me tell you something, some days
my secret parts are about as almond
as a wastewater treatment plant, but here he is,
lips puckered like a poet pursing for a pot pipe,
that's probably what he is, a poet, a pot pipe partaker,
wearing that funny hat he won't take off
for dinner, ink stained hands, no calluses,
a light in his eyes that would be
the knowing of me, another muse
bepedestalled and defenseless
a sculpture to be caressed coldly
and without reciprocation
like a shadow on the wall of a cave.

In the beginning

What appear to be different elementary particles
are actually different "notes" on a fundamental string.
The universe—being composed of an enormous number
of these vibrating strings—is akin to a cosmic symphony
– Brian Greene, The Elegant Universe

When God made the Universe
S/He made music. The Big Bang
nothing but a cosmic chord
on Marshall stacks turned up to eleven.
S/He made us all of vibrations,
fundamental notes inside the insides
of our insides' insides. Way down deep
like blues from the bottom of a black hole.
The stars, the planets, the air, the atoms,
the particles, the soul—all made
of Music. You will never die—
only become another movement—a fugue,
a riff, a drum roll, an operetta—
when you are old and afraid and feel it
coming, inhale: S/He is breathing
into you. Be not afraid. Be still. Listen.

Letter to a student, just before the Census, 2010

*"Our Government can learn anything about us
with just simply getting our full name and social security number"*
- from a student essay

Ah, Lisa, but do they know how the light in your eyes
turns on when your boyfriend squeezes you
on the loveseat? Do they understand why
you left school immediately when you learned
your sister was having her baby? So what
if they can track my credit card usage,
draw data from grocery card swipes.
Am I the sum of my purchases? Are you?
Does the fact that your mother had to apply
for Medicaid to push you into this world
in a well-lit room peopled with surgical masks
mean you'll be cooking meth by age 16? If
they know you're Methodist, do they really know
what you think of God? Is your grade
in Statistics and Probability proportionate
to how much of Him or Her or It
you think is possible, is real? Does your race,
gender, hair color, height, weight, level of education,
life expectancy and lifetime taxes paid
equal every part of you?
Lisa, in essence, are you not immeasurable?

Vagaries of Christendom

"What's he building in there?" my mom
asked my wife, but the 9-year-old answered.
"He's making a door to take the place
of the door that's there." I thought *damn*
and said: "Don't." "I wasn't," my wife said
"I was only thinking it," which means
she wasn't going to *say* she married a man
who can't make things, can't fix things.

The neighbor teaches History at the local
Christian college—I think he carpentries
to feel closer to Jesus—one time the Protestant drama teacher
at my school said, "I always imagine Him being *built*.
You know, working with *wood*." And there's another
thing I can't build—pictures of Jesus
in my mind, the iconography supplied
by my preferred Church (the One True, we claim—who doesn't?)
all sort of Eurocentric-y, non Jewish…
the long hair I believe, tho'—He's the biggest rockstar
the world has ever known, John Lennon's comments
notwithstanding—when He made the blind see can't you imagine
women Jew or Gentile asking Him to autograph their tits?

I've never rebuilt an engine either,
never plumbed the depths of the kitchen sink
like a blue collar philosopher who charges $60 minimum
just for showing up to contemplate faucets, didn't build
our one-year-old's birthday cake on the table
or the store-bought stuffed shells we ate for lunch
that third Sunday of Lent, March 7 of a season in which
I relinquished sodapop because the absence of beer in my life
is an impossibility at this juncture, like His presence
in the Host that morning is a Truth in my life
but at this juncture an impossibility in yours.

Margaret Hires a Personal Thinker

"If you cannot think well, others will do your thinking for you."
—George Orwell

It was always so...I don't know ...
middle class...all that weighing
of options...criticizing...do I take
a left turn here...is that really a good
movie...even when giving up control, one had to go
to *so* many sources to get one's thinking done
without effort...and its always ideological—
very Marxist, don't you think?...Even if one ultimately
chooses Fox News...and I've got
too much *money* to be a Marxist, honey...
I placed an ad in the *New Yorker*...very
discreet...Thinker Wanted, pay negotiable...
he showed up wearing an ascot, I hired him immediately...
Gustav does it all...the best part is
he doesn't even realize how much I should be paying him...
he chose my outfit this morning, do you like it?...
and made up my mind about that *Times* article...
those absolutely ghastly Democrats...he decided
I'm in favor of abolishing public education...
it's a failed experiment, really...an equalizer
that subverts itself and perpetuates the dominance of—
what was it?...but you see what I mean...
with Gustav, I'm brilliant...and I don't even have to try ...

Fundamental Truisms

They discovered Noah's Ark
again. For those of you
who aren't religious: a giant wooden ship
capable of containing all creatures
in twos. No big dinosaurs.
In the evangelical Christian women's group
my wife, a Catholic convert, attends
for the breakfast spread, a local Christian college
professor spoke, citing Biblical evidence
only for small dinosaurs. Thus,
no T-Rexes on the Ark. Neither
any huge plant-eating whateverasauruses.
I want to know: what did the lions eat?
Did they go vegan 40 days and long meatless nights?
Fast? Because no pair of zebras or giraffes
is lasting 40 days in close quarters with famished lions.
Maybe God insisted all the animals hibernate,
a decree the bears took to immediately. Maybe the speaker
at the mom's group, who answered one question
"I'm not a biologist, but ..." is right.
Maybe I'm no kind of Christian
without a blind trust that every word
of what they call the Word of God is true.

I can't wait until J.D. Salinger dies

and literary anthropologists armed with blacklights
and gold-panning sieves
break into his hideaway in—where is it?
a cabin on the side of a minor mountain in Maine
surrounded by black bears and barricaded
with the literary detritus of the last half
of the downward-spiraling 20th century—
that must be it, the place
where he keeps everything he's written
since retiring from publishing and pop culture,
out of agents' reach and editors' revisions,
himself revisioning visions of formerly hidden truths,
out there, beyond the siren call of celebrity,
past Caribbean Krakens and CGI-ejaculated Avatars,
notebook scribbling and typewriter typing
tomes of unknown wisdom, untold plots
and incessantly quirky characterization
left around the cabin like ore, like coals
squeezed into diamonds, like uranium
bursting with the exponential energy
to destroy videogames,
multitasking, social networking,
synergy, psychosomatic pharmaceutical plenitude
and restless leg syndrome
in one swell fffffffffffffffffffffffoop.

What would Jesus *really* do?

If He's turned down for a prom date
by the girl He's been working up courage to ask
since Homecoming, would He gaze skyward
crying My God, My God, Why Have You Forsaken Me?
Would He transform the severely autistic boy
she peer tutors in the special needs program
into a social genius who can work a room like Bill Clinton
just to impress her? Would she go to prom with that boy
instead of embracing the Way the Truth and the Life?
If He gets a flat on a county road after drinking too many beers
to drive home legally, would tire repair
be added to the list of His minor miracles?
Would Satan show up to tempt Him to change
his 98 Honda Civic into a tricked out Caddy with spinners?
If, technically, miracles weren't banned
from the Mermaid Festival 3 on 3 tournament
would He hit three pointers from Downtown—literally—
and check jumping from half court?
If He found an image of himself in a pancake at IHOP
would He sell it on Ebay, or otherwise
market waffle molds of His face
on infomercials like a new Glorified Shamwow Guy?
Would He also be disgraced in the pop cultural milieu
when arrested for consorting with prostitutes, too?

I killed J.D. Salinger

On the afternoon of Friday January 22nd 2010
I wrote a poem called "I can't wait
until J.D. Salinger dies." Less than
a week later, he was dead. It's true.
I have the dated email with the first poem,
sent to Kaveh one day before the death.
I feel karmically responsible.
Actually, I feel pretty good about it.
I didn't know I had
that kind of pull
in the universe.
In my next poem I'll be wishing
all cable tv political commentators
struck dumb. Also, I can't wait
until the Second Coming
of Walt Whitman, when he descends
from the clouds and proclaims me
his One True Poetic Descendent.

What? Like you wouldn't?

Dogmatics

The nun-Principal at Sacred Heart Elementary
told us one only need take communion
twice a year in the correct frame of mind
to enter heaven, which is why
a comedian can call her show "Jesus is Magic!"
so we can all laugh at Christians.

What is the right frame of mind, I wonder?
It must be a list of things one must not think
while ingesting the Host: don't imagine doggy style,
don't swear in your head, don't stare at the rear end
of the milf two rows up, don't plot revenge against those
to whom you should turn a cheek, above all don't disbelieve.

These dogmatic formulas for spiritual success
are the sketchy side of Catholicism, God as
the Almighty Dogmatician, adding up your acts of kindness,
subtracting for each time you've masturbated,
dividing by your divorce and multiplying
by your fruitful multiplying.

But I like a little mystery sprinkled over
my Catholic Crunch in the morning, grace
in the kind word to the kid who gets picked on,
grace in stopping to help the pizza guy fix a flat,
grace in treating one's spouse and children gently,
and the grace in raising one's eyes to heaven
on any given night of solitude or peace or good cheer
and saying thank you.

Analogies

A jiffy is to unit of time
as cubit is to unit of space.
Zoloft is to depression as cocaine
is also to depression. Billy Sunday
is to drinking as Glenn Beck is
to rational thinking. My frontal lobe
is able to withstand a nine-ale hangover
as my legs are able to run a 10K:
it can be done, but with an ostentatious
lack of grace. Grace under pressure
is to my moments of greatest stress
as miraculously multiplying thousand dollar bills
are to my wallet. Jesus is to Yahweh
is to Buddha is to Darwin is to John Lennon
as can't they all be right in their own way?
Would it really damn you to hell
or mute your hipster vibes permanently
to think somebody else's answers
might not be all wrong? If I compare
a pile of manure to extra virgin olive oil,
are you going to make salad dressing with it?
We can thank the Scholastic Aptitude Test
for this, transforming potential poets
into mere mathematicians of language.
When we all agree to call that manure
a pile of shit, then we can acknowledge
where our vegetables come from.
Then maybe death will be as unremarkable
as masticating the morsel on fork's end, as inevitable
as the finite and cacophonous movement
in the symphony that follows.

Choosing Day

When the time came,
we all shuffled to the cafeteria
as if we'd pick it out a la carte: fruit
or not? They brought us one by one
into a kind of voting booth, but larger—
drapery walls, a panel of adults:
a doctor, a teacher, a stoney-faced pastor—
all waiting for each pupil to choose.
This was fifth grade. I barely knew
which breakfast cereal to pick out
in the morning. They called me in and
I tried to stand straight, overcompensating
with shoulders thrown back like Freddie Mercury
pretending he can rock like a real man.
This was *the* choice. The one we all make,
the decision to cultivate heterosexual or
homosexual proclivities like a gardener
tending to a plant that will flower brilliantly,
overtaking even the heartiest weeds. I spoke too loud
when they asked, my voice cracked.
"HeterOsexual!" I proclaimed,
tripping on the O like a mic feeding back.
The pastor watched me carefully, let his ballpoint
drum against the table top. Shook
his head and asked, "Are you...sure?"

Scientific Curiosities

They're mapping Ozzy's genome
to determine how he's survived so long.
Why stop there? There's so much we can learn
from Celebrity Idiocy. Celebratology.
Better than American Studies because
it's a science, no mere humanity,
although we could study their humanity,
whether the starlets who adopt third world babies
are rescuing them or providing eye candy
for the paparazzi, the ruin and triumph
of Mickey Rourke, Dr. Drew exploiting the C list
because crack addicted adult child stars
make for great tv. Surely we could
find empirical explanation for the following:
how is Justin Bieber popular, why is Beck
a scientologist, and how long
until the book of Oprah is added to those
women's devotional Bibles?
We'll open a lab. Once the cable reality shows
about sex addiction and wedding cakes
and interventions and conniption fits won't have them,
they can sell their brains to us,
for study. Playing dude what would happen
with Abe Vigoda and unhealthy doses of Viagra,
or putting Ted Nugent on a leash
with a venison steak just out of reach.
Will he gnaw through a chain
to taste Bambi's flank?
There are so many unanswered questions,
like who wins a cage match
between Sacha Baron Cohen and Sean Hannity,
or what should one do
when given a chance at 36 hours naked
with a supermodel—male or female, take your pick—

which would result in a lifetime of fantasies during sex
with your otherwise frumpy mate,
but you'd be required to contract herpes
and circle your bicep with a tribal tattoo?

Duct Tape yer Windows, O ye Faithful

On the first day of the first week of the first month,
a thousand birds fell down dead from the Arkansas sky,
and on the second day, 100,000 fish washed up
dead on the shores of the Arkansas River. So, my friend,
are you still confident that the end ain't nigh?
Expect the next wave to be 10 million
Arkansite badgers stiffening forever in the cold,
mark my word, O ye most unholy pagan infidels.
The signs abound. Moreso than you might think.
Look at your internet news, where 85 AntiChrists
are walkin' around just as well-as-you-please,
devil-may-care, Polly-Wanna-Horseman-of-the-Apocalypse.
Everything means somethin', didn' you know?
For example: when I walked out of church
all speaking-in-tongues-tied from being caught up
by the spirit, I felt a tap on my shoulder
but *warnt nobody there.* I got spooked
so I fingered the cross on my chest, ain't no demon
a good cross-fingerin' won't dispel. But they are here,
and they are Legion. Not like the American. That's the good kind.
But listen: I'm a Christian. When it's a-rainin' frogs
and a-riverin' blood, come on over to my house.
I got a ten-year supply of freeze-dried food
and 500 gallons of water and guns—oh, do I got guns, boy—
and you're welcome to them, just so long as
you testify that you believe.

What I would hope I'd say to any of my wife's friends who offers to "do" me

Wow. That's really nice. Really, it is—
it makes me feel all fresh and young and wanted,
like a Budweiser with a born on date, or a really ripe cantaloupe,
but listen, I'm so psychologically Catholic
when I expel my vasectomized juices into my wife's
once-fertile womb, I feel guilty. When weeks
of children up at all hours and in our bed and awake at random times
between 9:30 and 5 AM force my body
to satisfy the biological imperative unwittingly with pleasantly vivid
REM cycles or at my own behest with my wits about me in ways I
won't describe in any other way than "all by my lonesome"
I feel guilty. When I imagine you naked, which I have
with your various womanly and inviting fleshy parts
I feel the flames of Hell licking at my ankles,
and though as a mammal I am hardwired
to propagate progeny all over the sidewalks and kiddie pools
of creation like some Ancient Mating Hero
of an Archetypal Savage Trailer Park Culture
I'm going to have to say—as I'm sure I would hear
from you if you were sober and from women too numerous to count
had I ever had a singles bar phase in my past, thank you
but no. I'm not virile, I'm not potent, most of the time I feel like
a wimpy man trapped in a wimpier man's body, it would surely
be over well before you'd want it to be—due, again,
to the body's jumpy reaction eventuated by weeks
upon weeks of privation necessitated by allowing our four children
to spent their fitful nights at home,
so I'm not going to be talked into it. This is for your own good,
and mine, and you'll come to your senses and thank me
the next time you see me—why? because...I've got herpes.

Holy? Matrimony

L—used to say J—'s eldest child
got twice the grandparents, twice the Christmas presents,
twice the love, then she made J—twice divorced
and his love was neither doubled nor halved
but left to expire like a banana forgotten
on a cabinet shelf. M—who edited
the crappy college litmag introduced himself
in writing classes as "happily? married"
because he wanted that question mark to be the seed
of desire of college girls for him. College girls never
paid me much attention, a blessing I think,
because the woman I impregnated before matriculating
became my wife without me ever facing
real temptation, although there was the one girl,
long black hair, art student, not particularly pretty
but interesting to look at and after looking so much
she began to wave and say "hi!" in a disarmingly
carefree way. S—found T—mouthhugging
M—P—who, ironically, has always been
a prick, but T—was psycho and we were
making odds on the year of the divorce
at the wedding. It was the dumbest wedding
in the world. No booze. A minister the groom's mom
insisted on for the betrothed nonbelievers. Everybody
got drunk at our place before the ceremony but
S—only got mad at the best man for it.
I had no best man, unless you count O—, who
married us after an online ordination,
and then when my brother D—made me best man
I was honored, but also felt like a douche. Mom cried
at his wedding, tears of joy for the union of two
Notre Dame graduates. Cried at mine too,
because the ceremony wasn't Catholic.

A Funny Thing Happened
on the Way to the Splashpark

We had to stop in Columbia City
on the way to the splashpark
to get the secret ingredient for my first
original homebrew recipe at a place
called Anytime Fitness. We pull into
the Walmart Plaza, I'm expecting
a health food store, but of course
there's the post-work rush hour of tight butts
grinding away at stairclimbers and a guy
with veined balloonmuscled biceps
bleached teeth and hair saying,
"You look lost!" "I'm looking for a place
that sells PB2," I say. "That's us!" he says,
flashing me a grin so white and powerful
it voted for David Duke—twice—
but that's not even the thing that happened,
which we saw when we just pulled in
to Plaza Drive off 109, this dude,
ballcap on high, big grin on his face,
a hop in his step, wearing cotton shorts
about mid thigh, tubes running
from inside the shorts to a big plastic bag
attached to his calf, the bag flopping around as he walks,
about 1/3rd full of dark yellow liquid—
look, I know nothing's funny
about having a colostomy bag, but I'm not even sure
if that's what it was, all the tubing appearing to run
up the front end of the shorts—him looking so happy
walking so springy like he's on a bipolar high
then when we're coming out of the Walmart Plaza
we notice the sign on the building he was walking beyond
read "Drug and Alcohol Treatment Center"
and that's probably not supposed to be funny either

but we thought it was—we drove around
looking for him with the camera ready
but didn't see him, so at this point
Bag-of-Piss-Man's existence is about as verifiable
as the existence of the Sasquatch
and only as believable as my word, in this,
one of the few poems I've written in which
every word is true.

I can't wait for the 2nd Coming

It'll be stealth—
Jesus flying in from Heaven undercover.
Setting up secret world domination headquarters
from a lair inside a dormant volcano.
Dismantling all nukes by washing the feet
of the Joint Chiefs of Staff unawares.
Making carbombs erupt into butterflies.
Granting unconditional freedom
to all heavenly Islamic virgins.
Laying hands on hamburgers,
making them moo again.
Soon crowned and mighty like no
Obama or Ahmadenijad could ever be.
Totally sweet for All God's People,
which is everybody. He'll turn water
into wine that enhances your liver,
break bread faster than rising from the dead
and hold one big hoedown hootenanny
like a true 60s-hippie-fest but
with better hygiene, miraculously
multiplying crab cakes and no brown acid.

Natural Behaviors

At the Denver zoo,
their enrichment department
encourages natural behaviors
in animals. For this same reason,
humans have bars. Why else
would a man who bumps another
spilling beer on two t-shirts
raise his arms and say "whut?!"
like a peacock strutting
rather than offer an apology,
a drink. Here's why:
that slim busty woman
atop a barstool looking
past him for her girlfriend
who he thought was checking
out the badass tribal
around his bicep. He says
"I was ridin' Harleys
when ridin' Harleys wasn't cool,"
which is at least two lies.
The woman sips her Roman Tea
holds her elbows in close
due to the female instinct
to take up as little space
as possible, though the lawyers
of biology and sociology
both claim this principle.
In Schools of Education
(hopelessly redundant institutions
like schools for the blind
who can't see), they claim
the male teenage homo sapiens
is willing to be rebuked
in private, but not in front of peers

for whom he puffs his chest
before clubbing a girl on the head
and dragging her off to a cave
to mate. In my first year teaching,
if I pulled a boy into the hall
to talk, Aristeo, the built-like-
a-brick-shithouse Mexican,
would pipe up, "they're havin'
a powwow!" and ridicule me
for keeping the write up
in the desk drawer.
What I'm trying to say is:
how the hell did men
get like this? Only women
and nonmasculine poets wonder,
but no one really knows. Not
Dr. Phil. Not Darwin.
Not Jesus Christ. Not even
Oprah. Even Nate,
who likes to say "I almost
beat his ass" all the time
even though he's never thrown
a punch, lays claim to his
beerfueled manliness before
his tendency to pick up bar tabs
out of sheer generosity.
I claim ignorance
in matters of the fist and gun
and only tip my bartenders—male
or female—well enough
to maintain courteous service
but not so much
that they think
I'm flirting with them.

Hunting for Groceries

Hear me, O great bag of Perdue™ brand chicken parts,
on this the day of your expiration
in this the bin of meats no tribesman
who drives a 40 thousand dollar stallion
comes near: I ask your permission
and the permission of the Great Spirit
that I might draw my wallet
out of my pants like a brave drawing an arrow
and purchase you
after swiping my grocery card, for which
your day-of-expiration manager's special sticker
will yield discounts in heavy abundance.
Allow me to marinate you in vinegar-heavy sauces
and barbecue you at temperatures from which
no flesh returns unscorched, so that I might
benefit from your proteins and B vitamins
while avoiding the sly maneuvers of classic tricksters
coyote, fox, and salmonella.
And six to twelve hours after I feast upon you
along with appropriately apportioned sides of roughage
and Cool Ranch Doritos™, may I have
abundant bowel movements of such volume
girth and gusto that the heavens shake with their thunder
and the earth we borrow from our children
sighs with delight upon the plopping.
And may I plop in humility and thanksgiving
for your gifts; and may I know no wisdom
but that which the voices of the ancients foretell
through the conduit of commentators
ordained to indicate down and distance
on HDTV, on a typical September Sunday afternoon.

Questions from the 33rd Hearing of the Associated Writing Programs Unpoetic Activities Committee

Are you a working class poet?
Have you ever considered yourself a working class poet?
Are you associated with any known working class poets?
Do you suspect any associates of being working class poets?
Are you aware that dressing up your subjects in denim and rags is
    as far as we'd like you to take it?
Do you knowingly pursue knowledge of the books of Edward Field,
Thomas McGrath, or Charles Bukowski? Have you had
    the opportunity to eliminate books by these poets? Have you
    eliminated them?
Do you believe that your poetry "career" is the most important
    aspect of your poetry? Are you willing to acquiesce to our views
    of what poetry is and ought to do and ought to be in order to
    further your "career"?
Do you believe in such as thing as the "bardic" tradition? Are
    there any traditions you feel the lyric tradition is secondary to?
Are you familiar with the views of such dangerous dissidents as
Linda McCarriston and Don Winter?
Which do you prefer—the life stories of the Romantic poets, or
    the trappings of Romantic poetry?
Do you believe identity with the working class trumps sympathy
    for the working class?
Do you drink to relieve the pressures of unemployment or the
    rote monotony of manual service and/or factory work that lacks
    complexity, autonomy, and the possibility of greater reward for
    greater effort?
Or do you drink to satisfy your idea of yourself as a poet?
Should a stripper in a poem be a heroin addict who dopes you
    up and steals your wallet, or a hooker with a heart of gold?
Do you see yourself or where you come from as disenfranchised
    in any way? If so, do you actually see that perception of
    disenfranchisement as legitimate?

Do you have any money in the bank?

Are you willing to let a panel of peers—our peers—you can think of it as a workshop—tell you what's wrong with your poetry? Are you willing to forgo any identification with working class ideology in favor of truth—our truth?

Online Headline: When Is It Alright To Masturbate in Public?

I don't know, but pretty soon
the damn progressives will pass a law
to make it alright never. When is it okay
to carry a concealed weapon into church?
Same answer. Why can't we just privatize education
and make the poor kids learn to read by deciphering
the warning label on a pack of menthol cigarettes
like a gosh damn Rosetta stone? If Planned Parenthood's
such a good idea, then why do we even
have a welfare system? Why shouldn't I call
your socialistic propaganda anti-American class warfare
when I'll fight to the death with my guns
for my $7.25 an hour assembly line job
with no benefits at Indiana Widgets? I want
our next President to be named Bill Smith.
I wanna win the lottery so I can build a bomb shelter
big as the new Jerusalem Revelations promises.
And for as long as we do still have public education,
I want every American schoolkid saying the Lord's Prayer
right before the Pledge of Allegiance in the morning,
just like George Washington and Thomas Jefferson did.

I'm from Indiana

I'm from Indiana and I'm not in the Klan.
I don't know anybody in the Klan. But years ago
they did have a sparsely populated Klan rally
on my hometown's courthouse steps where my ex-wife,
before I knew her, kicked a cop in the nuts.

I'm from Indiana and I don't think I'm from
the south. I don't speak with a drawl. I don't say
"warsh." I don't watch NASCAR. I don't spend
half the paycheck on lottery tickets, except on
the 4th of July, when I don't spend that lottery ticket money
on fireworks.

I'm from Indiana and I know Bobby Knight is not
Jesus. Larry Bird is not Jesus. Peyton Manning
is not Jesus. Mitch Daniels is the god-damn antichrist.
And yes, I pretty much think Jesus is Jesus—but I don't
get too carried away with that.

I'm from Indiana and I'm Catholic and where I'm from
in Indiana people think that means I've set up a shrine
to Mary in my basement where I burn incense and
sacrifice unbaptized babies and asphyxiate myself with a rosary
while "cleaning out the pipes."

I'm from Indiana and I will kick your ass
in a game of H-O-R-S-E.

I'm from Indiana and this guy I work with was Mr. Basketball
in 1985. He's a pretty cool guy. He said nice things
about my car, once.

I'm from Indiana and I don't hate black people.
I don't mind that all kinds of Hispanics are moving into

53

my neighborhood. Old Hoosiers whisper about it.
Big fucking deal. I'd rather have them around than the hicks
from Silver Lake who rent the house across the back yard
and who we think are cooking up and/or selling meth
and whose dog always humps our dog who sits there
and takes it until her fur is all gooey.

I'm from Indiana and I believe in equal rights for
gays. I don't hate atheists. I don't hate Christians.
One of my best friends is Mormon. I dislike hippies
because they're usually using the "kind brother" routine
to get into somebody's pants. I try not to be an asshole.
Sometimes I am anyway.

I'm from Indiana and I have no idea how to cultivate
an ear of corn, impregnate a cow, or churn butter.

I'm from Indiana and I know all the words to
"Back Home Again in Indiana," but this is not
the Indianapolis 500 and I am not going to sing it for you now.

The Guy Who Heard the Call

They ran a story in the South Bend Trib
about a guy standing 6 hours daily in 10 degree weather
on a busy streetcorner waving around a Ziploc-wrapped
King James Bible at cars because
God told him to. Listen, you don't have to preach
to convince me God's ways are not Man's ways,
His/Her/Its Will a mystery wrapped in a conundrum
topped with Tobasco chased with Pepto—but
if this is God's marketing plan
He really oughta hire a p.r. firm!
Is it a solo decision? The Almighty longly leaning
from on High into the ear of an unemployed truck driver
in Arctic Indiana, commanding *not here, not here, not here,*
now stop. This be the place.
Get out the Word. Start shouting. I have to believe
this is the work of a committee, because
all the worst decisions are made by committees
and for all we know God is not really a "Him" but
a committee, which would make anthrax, terrorism,
and Alfonso Soriano's contract that much more understandable
        —as Heavenly missives, anyway, as mysteries,
workings within workings, some flunkie angel go-fer
who fetches coffee for the Omniscient Collective
sent down to whisper in that poor man's ear:
Now get out your book. Wave it around. Smile. They want you
to look like you're having fun…and/or batshit crazy.
God usually speaks to us in more subtle ways these days, unless
you're Pat Robertson, whose back yard is all lit up with the Burning Bushes
he'd like to toss the gays into, but let's assume momentarily
the voice the man heard was The Voice, not just a fragment
of the spiraling monologue we all carry in our heads—would you respond,
"Here I am, Lord. I have heard You calling." Or would it be,
"I'm not the one, Lord. I'd rather burn in Hell than suffer out in this cold."

At Verizon Wireless

Why do I always
get the new guy?
Had to replace my wife's phone,
which our 16-month-old son,
a future Olympian discus thrower,
likes to practice with, and
new guy called in boss because
he couldn't get the broken phone
to turn on, then boss and new guy
hold a powwow in that room
they scan id's to get into
—God knows what they have
back there, probably Mother Mary's
Magic Undies and pieces
of the True Cross—boss comes out
and says the screen is scratched so
the warranty "don't count," that's
the way he said it, "it don't count"
then when I'm asking new guy questions like
"what's the cheapest reliable phone we can use
to talk and text" he's asking questions like
"that depends—do you want a Camaro
or a Pinto?" and I hate Camaros—
show me the Camaro driver whose not closely
in touch with his inner douchebag—
he points to a phone next to a sign reading
"$59.99 after rebate" and says
"this can do so much more!" than
the one I'm pointing at
which reads "$19.99 after rebate"
and I say "can we talk and text
on this one?" him: yeah
me: then I'm going with the Pinto.
Then he tries to sell me insurance

because we've both learned from boss
that when a broken phone under warranty
is brought in, the warranty "don't count"
he tells me if we break this one
we'll have to sacrifice our discus-
throwing son to a demon of the underworld
of the 27th order or take out
a home equity loan to replace it,
I can't remember which,
then I have to stand there while he takes
40 minutes to download what
is necessary onto the phone,
during which I have a gloriously elaborate
and mostly yellow fantasy
of pissing on everything
in the store—the computer terminals,
the gray carpet, the back room
with the secret stores of plutonium-
enriched french ticklers, the $500
phones that will live your life for you
except better than you can,
the shirts and ties and pinstripe pants
of the salesmen, my penis a firehose
my intent to wash clean like the God
of Noah, only there will be no rainbow,
no promise of pardoning all future pissings
for the penance of 40 days and dropped call nights
awash on an ocean of piss, only
a two year service agreement,
and a monthly bill I will continue
to pay using an envelope and postage stamp.

Paths to Nirvana

Mom: they claim Kurt Cobain
did heroin to self-medicate
chronic stomach problems. Do you mind
if I start mainlining crystal meth
to treat my chronic fatigue?
I also have restless leg syndrome.
I think amputation is probably
the best route to recovery. I know I'm 34
and hardly ever ask for advice anymore
but you give it freely enough
so in your experience…your infinite
wisdom, having no experience—in your sentience…
in your half asleep insomnia watching Larry King
lurch into your bedroom from 3000 miles away
like the stretchy creepy male cougar he is,
I want to say: I've been depressed
lately. Do you think periodical
nosefuls of cocaine will cure me?

Poem, USDA Inspected and Approved

Lady Gaga wore a dress made of meat
to an awards show and if it's true
for every action there is an equal and opposite reaction
then somewhere someone is eating a steak
made of fabric. There are public service announcements
advising the youth of America not to
wear meat dresses this cold Halloween weekend
because it may result in hypothermia.
There's no mention of other results such as:
1. popularity with dogs
2. spontaneous eruptions of NRA meetings
3. Ew.
Lady Gaga calls her rabid fans little monsters
and by rabid I mean foaming at the mouth
and by monster she means album-and-ticket-purchasing
public citizen. I like Lady Gaga, or the idea of Lady Gaga,
my idea of Lady Gaga, as what I imagine outweighs
what I know though I'm not one to imagine her
with simultaneous man parts and woman parts. Ew.
(Sorry, hermaphrodites.)
                        There's a hallway to the moon
and Lady Gaga takes my hand and walks me through
and when we reach the top the moon is made
of Vegan cheese, which is made of something that grows
not something that moos. We waltz. She kisses me by
sexually. When she abandons me like a little monster
without a closet I frump down into the vegancheesedust
looking down at Earth lonely for everyone
thinking *is that the Great Wall of China?* and also
what an impressive view.

The Voice of God Told Me Agnosticism Is the One True Faith

It spoke to me from a cloud
or it didn't, It spoke from the sky (perhaps),
It might've spoken from a burning bush,
It might've made a rainbow in the sky
I couldn't see, It might've sent Its perfect children
to save you and me, It might've died,
It might've rose, It might be fake,
oh thar she blows, It might've said
I am a Lie, It might've said
you'll never die, It might be dead
like Nietzsche said, It might live
in the broken bread, I might be sure
but really not, I could be wrong
I'm wrong a lot

What a Drag It Was That One Time When the Emperor from *Star Wars* Showed Up at Our Labor Day Barbecue

And we're all "it's not a costume party, dude"
and he's all "soon you will see that it is you
who are mistaken—about a *great many things*!"
and we're all "suit yourself. You want a beer?"
and he's all "it is I who allowed the rebel spies
to learn the location of the Death Star!"
and we're all "Ummmm…so it's pretty much
burgers and brats, you're not vegetarian,
are you?" and he's all
"a brat would do quite nicely, thank you"
and we're all "do you prefer kinda charred
or a little red in the middle—we can't help it,
Mike's on the grill, he's an idiot"
and he's all "soon you will come to know the True Power
of the Dark Side!" and we're all
"ok! charred it is!" and then after he eats
we're all "wanna play some Cornhole?"
and he's all "your friends will not survive!"
and we're all "you sound like Dave—he always talks smack
then throws a hissyfit when he loses" and then Dave's all
"I'm not with you, wrinkly old man.
I'm not pairing up with you." and the emperor's all
"then *you will die*!" and he starts shooting lightning bolts
out of his fingers at Dave until Tiny—
you know Tiny? he's like 6'6", 280—
he picks up the emperor from behind and *throws* him
a sinkhole opens up, he *falls in*—yeah. weird. cosmic.—
like some Force that controls the universe wanted
to be rid of him—he hollered as he fell,
it sounded like a long way,
we didn't even hear him hit bottom—
then we called Nipsco, there was a gas line
exposed, and somebody's gotta clean *that* up,
but it wasn't gonna be me.

God's Plan

Protestants like to talk about God's Plan
but it's probably not having a cookout on Good Friday
which is why we can't, the epiphany after
our hasty party planning going like this:
"Wait: We're Catholic." Salmon fillets
were off limits, my wife gastrointestinally opposed
to gilled animals, so too Cornhole
and getting drunk semi-publicly in the back yard
because according to God: "my Son died today.
Don't enjoy yourself"—and also
what would the neighbors say? Probably
Good Giddilly Golly, them? Catholics
put the dog in dogma. They'd like to say
"the beef" but "Beefma" makes even
less sense. Then they'd call the cops on us
which really happened once for failing to detain
our small fast mutts who love the opportunity presented
by a cracked-open screen door like Paul
(formerly known as Saul) loved the opportunity
presented by an unconverted Gentile. Then
we'd lumber down the street as if bearing
a cross for someone else and use the Lord's name
in vain liberally while the conservative Protestant neighbors
accuse us the Pope and the local priest of abuse
of All God's Creatures Great and Small, from Altarboys
to Zoomonkeys, which might be suitable, not as an accusation
but as a transgression because then we'd all need properly forgiven.

Ode to my rockpants

Verily, O my rockpants, hearken unto my words
for time nears the month of poetry, and
I heartily have missed you. You whom I wore
at every band practice, and all six gigs.
You who were there when we played with
Joe's Garage, when we played with Bourbon Backroads Band,
and when we played with ourselves. For unto Heaven,
mighty rockpants, I declare that I have worn you
while playing with myself. I rejoice upon thy
canvassy material, which looketh like jeans, but are
not jeans, for I don't wear jeans, for they make my butt
look big. I have splotched paint upon thee
during Home Improvement Escapades. I have
prayed thanks for thine comfort fit waist,
in which I still fit after gaining eight pounds.
I have fallen in love with the seamstress
who hath fixed thine zipper, O my rockpants,
due to sundry imaginings of her strong fingers
deftly manipulating thine crotch.
But O rockpants, howuntofore my band
hath practiced not and gigged not, I proclaim
upon your repair you shall not fall into disuse.
You shall be worn at poetry shows.
You shall be worn on Nights Out. In splendor
you shall cover my big ass, in perpetuity
shall I crumple thee upon the bedroom floor
for you, O my beautiful rockpants, complete me.

17 Ways to Accidentally Off Your Child

Play truth or dare with your five year old,
an outlet, and a fork. Leave the carseat
on top of the car right before the demolition
derby. Put her on the roof and tell her
if she believes hard enough she can fly.
Mix his formula in your used meth lab equipment.
Give him a claymore and tell him to go slay a dragon
in a thunderstorm. Force feed her like a duck
then eat her liver. Let her play Frogger
on the freeway. Cut him in half
with the razor sharp wit of a douchebag
who writes poems about harming children.
Berate her until she loses hope.
Trade her to a stranger for a .30 aught 6.
Homemade rollercoaster. Let him play
infomercial man with a set of Ginsu knives.
Or just slice him and dice him yourself.
When you cook dinner for her grandparents
on their anniversary, tell them
they're eating her. Drop him
in a teabagger convention holding a copy
of the Communist Manifesto. Announce
she's an evangelical Christian in a room crowded
with rabid progressives. Give up feeding him for Lent.
When the cops come blame it on Jesus. When the Christians
can't forgive you make vows to the Devil.
When the Devil says too much for me,
all I do is rake in souls for giving folks the ability
to play a mean blues guitar, then know
that yours is the only solitary one on earth,
a soul that can't be saved, bargained for,
or given away, having given away
its last ounce of humanity and left to shrivel
like an unsuckled breast.

Staycation

Whenever I'm on vacation
I'm on vacation at home
because I can't afford vacation away from home
and this is called a staycation.
And I can't treat it like a trip to Vegas
because what happens in the home never leaves.
No matter how much I want to
this winter staycation,
I can't treat my wife like a prostitute.
I can train my children to bring me drinks
while I throw dice, but it makes me feel seedy
and besides we'd all rather play Twister without gambling
on left foot yellow or who falls first.
We can't drive cross country to Wally World
but we can usher the Griswolds into our living room
straight off the tv via the magic of Comcast On Demand.
This is paltry compensation for the hours of labor
through which I toil, for credit card Christmas purchases
paid off with the tax check, not to mention
the made-to-scale replica of the Great Pyramids
my heart holds in its own heart, deep
beneath the steely solemnity of the sternum.
On a tv staycation once Dr. Huxtable
put potato chips on a sandwich. I'm willing to get just about
that crazy, which means chasing a bowl of vanilla ice cream
with a home-brewed stout, or taking video
of our single-digit-aged children
drunk on hot chocolate reciting their fantastic bucket lists.

Note to my Atheist Friends (who will be coming over for a party)

for T. and J.

Hopefully when you see the crucifix
on the wall you won't start hissing
and clawing at the air like vampires or burst
into flame like the damned
or start quoting Richard Dawkins liberally
(surely not conservatively) or play quote-
the-famous-atheist like some people play
quote-the-Bible, like Wheel of Fortune,
spinning through verses and taking a guess,
seeing what sticks.
                    The fact that we don't know
if God is   is not proof
of His/Her/Its/Their inexistence
nor existence, but I do know
this: R—, in whose honor we hold the party,
is bringing his cheeseballs and they will be fantastic
and Jo— will tell true stories that no one believes in
and someone's child will behave badly
either once or always (I'm not a prophet,
you know) and C— will laugh awkwardly
and T—will kindly point it out
and I will fill my hollow soul
with two to eight twelve ounce beers, depending
on exactly how certain I am of my belief
that given night, and my wife
will apologize for things that aren't wrong
and in all these and more I have everlasting faith.

They Hoosier Play

Out of pick and roll
Out of drop step
Out of make it take it they Hoosier play

Out of take a charge
Out of blocking foul
Out of knee brace and ankle brace they Hoosier play

Out of 3 on 3 tournament
Mermaid Festival to Mentone Egg
Out of concrete court and Field House
Out of church gym and YMCA they Hoosier play

Out of sectional draw
Out of local radio play by play
With thunderstruck facepainted roaring fans they Hoosier play

With locked elbow and follow through
With nothin' but net
Boxed out and over the back they Hoosier play

With technical foul
With two free throws and two seconds left
With bragging rights for high school pals they Hoosier play

Out of glass backboards and wooden backboards
Out of Chuck Taylors and Air Jordans
Dripping sweat and sucking wind they Hoosier play

Further Evidence that Jesus Is the Answer

Q: To be or not to be?
A: Jesus Christ.

Q: When did you stop beating your wife?
A: Jesus Christ!

Q: What's for dinner?*
A: Jesus Christ.

Q: $(5n^2 + 3n)/13 = 42$ solve for n
A: n = Jesus Christ.

Q: A train is travelling west from Toledo at 70 mph, etc.
A: Jesus Christ.

Q: Why don't we do it in the road?
A: Jesus Christ.

Q: I'm sorry, can you repeat the question?
A: Jesus Christ?

*This is a Catholic question.**

Oh, come on, take it easy. *I'm* Catholic, bucko.*

***More accurately, I was at the time I wrote this poem.

Pig Spill

"50 Hogs Die When Semi Flips…"
                    —*headline, Warsaw Times-Union*

Chaos on US 30 tonight
when a fleet of animal carriers
tipped over due to a sudden 125 mph
gust of southerly wind resulting in
the Midwest's largest pig spill to date.
Meateating activists PorkPiece
are already on the scene waving placards
and burning vegetables in protest of what they call
a sure and serious hit to the Midwestern supply
of hamhocks and side meat, to say nothing
of the effect on the Canadian Bacon market.
The spill is so large it threatens surrounding
Natural Automotive Habitats, with live oinkers
running around area highways and byways like bumper cars
squealing and threatening to re-enact the Bolshevik revolution.
The danger to automobiles is so great, endangered species
like Toyotas That Brake on Command or
Babe Magnet Volvos are threatened.
Porky's Pork and Pork-Related Products, also
known in the industry as "Big Pig" and owners
of the fleet, pledge to do "everything in our
'the other white' power to rectify this matter."
Volunteers from a nearby barbecue sauce plant
are being recruited to canvas the area
in search of Rogue Animals-Made-of-Spareribs
and are being told to marinate on sight.

Prophecy

"Things are speeding up here in the end"
　　　　　　　—character in the movie Slacker

I think they're called fundamentalists
because they have a fundamental inability
to understand metaphor. That
"they shall take up serpents" isn't so much
a recommendation as a suggestion through faith
no harm will be done their eternal souls.
We all know bodies are born
to decay. Many don't know
the New Jerusalem Revelations promises
is more about politics in the time
of St. John of Patmos than
a huge city falling out of the sky
where everyone goes to Christian discos
and Billy Sunday bars flow with unending O'Doul's.
If no one knows the hour then why
are all you yahoos yammering on
about the End Times nigh? It's a theme
as old as five seconds after Christ died.
They say be ready for it anytime
but that's gotta work hell on your adrenal glands.
I'm a poet so when I look at the sky
it's not so much in anticipation
usually just to contemplate the moon.

Drinking Song

Mom poured Dad one Stroh's nightly,
can to frosty mug. Once, while watching her eyes
for disapproval, he announced he'd have a second and did,
offered a sip to me, asking for another,
even as Mom insisted, "It's an *acquired* taste"
using the word *acquired* in the same tone she'd say,
"That's *different*," for people's actions Dad
would proclaim *asinine*. Even then I understood
Dad needed beer, felt a right to it,
one nightly with Wheat Thin crackers
and the Warsaw *Times-Union*, a deal struck
with a cardiologist after the heart attack
that didn't kill him, before all that research
into the heart-healthiness of a single glass of red wine, daily.
After some experience sullying the waters
of my bloodstream with alcohol, I bragged to Mom
that he was never that kind of drinker, knew when
to say when, she said it wasn't always that way,
recounting the public singing and standing upon tables
in an Indianapolis bar, before they had kids.

How you define alcoholic
determines if I am, drinking daily, yes,
to relieve stress, often, to get hammered, rarely,
to help me love the moment when life's tedium
conspires against me, sometimes, with a sense
of gratitude for the first taste, always,
hitting rock bottom or getting a DUI or taking
a hangover sick day, never, never, and never.

My son, one year old, will point at the beer
in my hand and say "Daddy" as if the drink
is as natural an extension of me as the breasts

of his mother, her waters expressed to sustain
his life, my poison ingested, rationalized
as necessary, his dad like his grandfather,
God knows like any number of our Irish
and German forebears, claiming the habit
as our own, wanting never to give it up.

Why I'm Catholic (which is a word that means universal)

I don't pray to a theoretical God.
I don't pray to a Force
that can be used to lift starfighters
out of swamps if one concentrates
hard enough, or to an abstract nonentity
responsible for karma and the unification
of all Fields, such as: rugby,
gravitational, and Marshall.
Neither do I pray to an old man
with a flowing white beard on a throne,
with crown and scepter in the sky, a king
of kings, a literal Almighty Father.
I believe Jesus meant Father
metaphorically, something everyone
could understand in his day,
but these days God-the-Sandra-Day-O'Connor
is at least as metaphorically fitting.
Still I don't pray to a theoretical God.
Sometimes I imagine a Sacha Baron Cohen God.
Other times, Sylvester Stallone. Others,
a God who is a member of A Tribe
Called Quest. A Stephen Hawking God. A God
who stands in a crowd at a Phish concert
asking for spare change. All these inherently inadequate
because who understands Him or Her or It
when the entirety of HimHerIt is beyond human understanding.
In one of our puny attempts to make sense
of the universe our parish priest said
when God became Man it was like you or I
turning into a rock. That's how much
He lowered Himself. Although my rock brain
can only feebly attempt to know what is,
I believe that God is out there in here and all around,
and became Man to find an answer to the human question
How does it feel to be on your own?

Zombie Vegetarians Decimate California Field of Organic Bell Peppers

A bloodthirsty horde of zombie vegetarians
slouched out of Los Angeles nightclubs at 6 a.m., toward
a field of bell peppers, overpowering day laborers
to mutilate the entire crop, showing no mercy for the undergrown,
the stunted, or the rotting. Only gruesome shards
of seeds and stems remained.
One particularly dedicated supervisor
due a season-ending bonus
for the crop's high yield offered
his pinky fingers in exchange for the preservation
of the peppers, but the zombies simply shifted
their hemp cloth overalls and sidestepped the boss
with deft manipulations of their Birkenstocks.
Workers report that upon the brutal extinction
of the crop, the zombies began chanting,
"Me Want Half Decaf Soy Latte!…Me Want Chai!" whilst shuffling
toward San Francisco. On Cable News Talk TV today
Al Sharpton claimed the zombies organized
against racial discrimination, while Al Gore
claimed the appearance of the creatures
was an unforeseen result of the melting of the polar ice caps.
Meanwhile, on the 700 Club, Pat Robertson declared,
"Zombie Vegetarians? Here? Well then…God must hate gay people."

Nothing Is Sacred

We come together today to celebrate
Nothing, which is sacred. We come from Nothing
And we return to Nothing. We were made
by Nothing, and when we were made Nothing
had nothing in mind. Nothing provides No Place
for us to go after we die, unless we live
with too much of Something. In that case,
Nothing sends us No Other Place to live out
No Time At All. Nothing did not send Anything
to atone for the Something of mankind;
neither does Nothing spoken nor written tell us
something about Anything. So life continues,
for a time. Nothing will provide.

About the Author

Steve Henn doesn't think you should be too sure about anything.

The New York Quarterly Foundation, Inc.

New York, New York

Poetry
Magazine

Since 1969

Edgy, fresh, groundbreaking, eclectic—voices from all walks of life.

Definitely NOT your mama's poetry magazine!

The *New York Quarterly* has been defining the term contemporary American poetry since its first craft interview with W. H. Auden.

Interviews • Essays • and of course, lots of poems.

www.nyquarterly.org

No contest! That's correct, NYQ Books are NO CONTEST to other small presses because we do not support ourselves through contests. Our books are carefully selected by invitation only, so you know that NYQ Books are produced with the same editorial integrity as the magazine that has brought you the most eclectic contemporary American poetry since 1969.

Books

nyqbooks.org

CPSIA information can be obtained at www.ICGtesting.com
Printed in the USA
LVOW042148070912

297929LV00002B/1/P